Choices

By Dianne Irving

Pearson Australia
(a division of Pearson Australia Group Pty Ltd)
707 Collins Street, Melbourne, Victoria 3008
PO Box 23360, Melbourne, Victoria 8012
www.pearson.com.au

First published 2014 by Pearson Australia
2021 2020 2019 2018
10 9 8 7 6 5 4 3 2 1

Publisher: Dian Faulisi
Project Managers: Tamara D'Mello Pirois and Emma-Jane McCarroll
Editor: Philip Bryan
Cover and Series Designers: Jenny Grigg and Anne Donald
Designer: Norma van Rees
Copyright and Pictures Editor: Katy Murenu
Mac Operator: Rob Curulli
Illustrator: Fiona Lee
Printed in Australia by the SOS Print + Media Group

ISBN 978 1 4860 0856 8
Pearson Australia Group Pty Ltd ABN 40 004 245 943

Acknowledgements
We would like to thank the following for permission to reproduce copyright material.
The following abbreviations are used in this list: t = top, b = bottom, l = left, r = right, c = centre.

Alamy: JanuaryFrost, p. 17.
Corbis: Antoine Arraou, p. 14.
Fotolia: fotoschab, front cover; frank peters, back cover; pp. 3, 4(all), 10bl, 11r, 12r, 13b, 29; bob, p. 8tr; Okea, p. 6; oriori, p. 8cr; Alistair Berg, p. 10r; Sergey Khamidulin, p. 11l; kameel, p. 12b; raptorcaptor, p. 15; sooksun, p. 18; Stephen Finn, p. 21r; chrisdorney, p. 21l; Gudellaphoto, p. 22; DeVIce, p. 24; Monkey Business, p. 28; Monkey Business, p. 30.
Getty Images: Andersen Ross, p. 13r; Clark and Company, p. 20.
Pearson Australia: Alice McBroom, p. 7; Siân Bradfield, p. 9(all).

Every effort has been made to trace and acknowledge copyright. However, if any infringement has occurred, the publishers tender their apologies and invite the copyright holders to contact them.

Disclaimer
Some of the images used in *Choices* might have associations with deceased Indigenous Australians. Please be aware that these images might cause sadness or distress in Aboriginal or Torres Strait Islander communities.

Contents

Decisions

Everyday we make decisions, from the time we wake up to the time we go to bed. Some of these decisions are easy, but some are not so easy.

As we get older, we have to start making more decisions for ourselves. We need to make choices for our health, safety and wellbeing.

Sometimes the decision-making process can be hard because we don't have the right information. Sometimes it is hard because of pressure from other people. Other times it's hard because the right thing to do isn't always the easiest thing to do!

However, there are things we can do that make it easier to make decisions that are best for us. It is important to have knowledge about things that affect us and know what the **consequences** of our choices might be. It is important to recognise that you have a choice in the decisions you make: there are different options you can choose. It is also important to develop confidence in your decisions.

LET'S FIND OUT

- What choices can we make to keep ourselves healthy and safe?
- How do food labels make it easier to choose a healthy option?
- Do I need to increase the amount of exercise I do each day?
- What are the side effects of medicine, alcohol and tobacco?
- How can I say 'no' to harmful choices?

We need to make a range of decisions every day.
Some of these decisions are easier than others.

Making healthy food choices

Making good food choices is important for keeping our body healthy, so we get all the **nutrients** our body needs to **function** at its best. If our body is healthy, we are able to work better and play better.

Look at the labels

One way we can make a healthy and safe choice about the food we eat is by looking at food labels. Some food packaging tries to suggest that the food inside is very healthy, but don't let that trick you! It is always important to take a closer look at what's inside the product. Sometimes packaging will say 'low in fat', but the food might be very high in sugars or sodium instead. (Sodium is part of salt.) Or the packaging might say 'no added sugar', but it may have a high fat content.

It is always a good idea to check what is really in the food you are eating.

In Australia, there are rules about labels that have to be included on food packaging. Two labels that can be very helpful are the list of ingredients and the **nutrition** information panel.

This chart shows the percentage of foods you should eat daily from each group.

Ingredients list

Ingredients are listed in order of how much they weigh, from heaviest to lightest. So if sugar is the first ingredient on the list, you know that sugar is the main ingredient in that food. These lists can help us decide if a food is right for us, especially if we have food **allergies** or special **dietary** needs.

Looking at the first three ingredients on the list can help you make sure foods are not high in saturated fats, sodium or sugars. Sometimes ingredients have a percentage next to them, which gives even more information about how much of a specific ingredient is in the product.

Changing names

Be careful. Sometimes food ingredients are listed under different names!

Ingredients high in saturated fat can also be labelled as animal fat, butter, coconut oil, cream, dripping, lard, chocolate, palm oil, milk solids and vegetable shortening.

Other names for added sugar include dextrose, fructose, glucose, honey, maple syrup, golden syrup, lactose and sucrose.

Ingredients high in sodium might be labelled as baking powder, garlic salt, yeast extract, MSG, stock cubes or sodium nitrate.

INGREDIENTS

WHOLEGRAIN CEREALS (48%) [UNCLE TOBYS ROLLED **OATS** (37%), WHOLE **WHEAT** (11%)] RAW SUGAR, PUFFED RICE, VEGETABLE OIL [EMULSIFIER (**SOY** LECITHIN), ANTIOXIDANTS (304, 306)], MIXED NUTS (7%) [**CASHEWS, PECANS, ALMONDS, MACADAMIAS**], GLUCOSE (**WHEAT**), HONEY, COCONUT, DIETARY FIBRE (INULIN), TAPIOCA STARCH, SALT, SODIUM BICARBONATE, FLAVOUR, EMULSIFIER (**SOY** LECITHIN).

CONTAINS OATS, WHEAT, TREE NUTS AND SOY AS INDICATED IN BOLD TYPE. PRODUCT PROCESSED ON A LINE THAT ALSO PROCESSESS PRODUCTS CONTAINING MILK.

NUTRITION INFORMATION#

Servings per Package: 6 Serving Size: 20g (1 bar)

	Quantity per Serving	%Daily Intake* per Serving	Quantity per 100g
ENERGY	370kJ	4%	1840kJ
PROTEIN	1.7g	3%	8.3g
FAT, TOTAL	3.2g	5%	16.2g
- SATURATED	0.7g	3%	3.5g
CARBOHYDRATE	12.0g	4%	60.1g
- SUGARS	3.4g	4%	16.8g
DIETARY FIBRE	1.7g	6%	8.6g
SODIUM	55mg	2%	265mg

All specified values are averages
*Percentage Daily Intakes are based on the average adult diet of 8700kJ. Your daily intakes may be higher or lower depending on your energy needs.

The list of ingredients and the nutrition panel provide detail about the food contents.

Nutrition information panel

The nutrition information panel must list the amount of energy (kilojoules), protein, fat, carbohydrate and sodium in the food. The panel lists the information per serve and per 100 g (or per 100 mL for liquids). The serving size can help you work out how much of each nutrient you are getting – but check to make sure your serve is the same size as the serve on the label!

Energy and kilojoules

Energy from food is measured in kilojoules. If we don't get enough energy, our bodies won't function properly. If we get too much, the extra energy may be stored as fat.

Protein

Protein is needed to grow and develop. It helps our bodies repair cells and make new ones. **Lean** meat, eggs, fish, dairy products and legumes are great sources of protein.

Fat

Fat is necessary for good health. Some fats are healthier than others. Saturated fats can increase our risk of heart disease, and we should limit these in our diet. The nutrition panel lists the total amount of fat, as well as the amount of saturated fats. Eating avocados and nuts is a good way to get healthy fats.

The serving size on the nutrition panel should be used as a guide.

Carbohydrates

Carbohydrates are the main way we get energy for our bodies. Protein and fat also give us energy, but it is the energy we get from carbohydrates that our body uses first.

Sugars are a type of carbohydrate. They include natural sugars that can be found in some foods like fruit, as well as added sugars. Sugars are included in the total carbohydrate amount, as well as being listed separately.

Some good food choices for carbohydrates include fruit, wholemeal bread and pasta, rice, and wholegrain breakfast cereals.

Sodium

Sodium is the part of salt that can cause health problems. Too much sodium can lead to high blood pressure or a stroke.

Comparing products

Often the serving size for two foods is not the same, so if you are **comparing** two foods, it's best to use the information in the 100 g listing. Try to choose the food that is lowest in fat, sugars and sodium.

Did you know?

The salt we eat is called sodium chloride, which is a chemical compound made up of sodium and chlorine.

AUSTRALIAN NUTRITION INFORMATION
Servings per package: 2.5 • Serving size: 40 g

	Average Quantity per 40 g Serving	Average Quantity per 100 g
Energy	860 kJ/ 208 kcal	2150 kJ/ 520 kcal
Protein	2.8 g	7 g
Fat, total	14.0 g	35 g
- saturated	6.8 g	17 g
Carbohydrate, total	17.2 g	43 g
- sugars	16.8 g	42 g
Sodium	12 mg	30 mg

NUTRITION INFORMATION
Servings Per Pack: 5 Serving Size: 100g

Average Quantity:	Per Serve	Per 100g
ENERGY	270kJ	270kJ
PROTEIN	5.7g	5.7g
*FAT TOTAL	0.15g	0.15g
- SATURATED	0.09g	0.09g
- TRANS	0.01g	0.01g
CHOLESTEROL	0.7mg	0.7mg
CARBOHYDRATES TOTAL	7.5g	7.5g
- DIETARY FIBRE	0.2g	0.2g
- SUGAR	6.1g	6.1g
SODIUM	53mg	53mg
GLUTEN	0mg	0mg
CALCIUM	220mg (27% RDI)	220mg (27% RDI)#

#Percentage of recommended dietary intake.

Read the information in the 100 g column to compare two different products.

Choosing physical activity

Children and teenagers who are active are usually healthier and happier because they are more energetic and they are less **stressed**. They can meet new friends, their bones and muscles are stronger, they are more confident, more relaxed and they sleep better.

The Australian Government **recommendation** is that children get 60 minutes of moderate to vigorous physical activity every day. But don't worry; it doesn't all have to be at once. It can be spread out over the whole day! If you can include an activity that lasts for 10 to 15 minutes, that will be great for your heart rate. Moderate exercise includes things like walking, riding a bike, skateboarding or dancing. A vigorous activity could include running, swimming laps, training for a sport – or anything that raises your heart rate. If you can, it is great to include at least 20 minutes of vigorous activity three or four times a week.

Did you know?
It is an Australian Government recommendation that children should not spend more than two hours a day using electronic media. That includes computer games, television and the Internet.

Aim for 20 minutes of vigorous activity several times a week.

Happy and confident

Exercise can make you feel happier and more confident. During exercise, our brain releases chemicals, such as endorphins and dopamine, which make you feel happy and more relaxed. You may also feel very proud of your **achievements**, which can help you feel more confident. Exercising can help take your mind off anything that is worrying by giving you something else to **concentrate** on.

More energetic

Exercise can make you more energetic because it **improves** your fitness. It can make your muscles stronger and able to work for longer periods of time without feeling tired. Your heart can become stronger, making it able to pump blood around your body faster and with less effort. Everyday tasks become easier, as well as things that take a bit more effort, like hiking up a hill.

Healthy body weight

Being active helps you control your body weight. A healthy body weight reduces your risk of getting diseases such as type 2 diabetes, heart disease and heart problems. It can also help you feel better about yourself!

Better sleep

Some studies have shown that people who exercise fall asleep faster and have a deeper sleep. That means you wake up feeling more refreshed in the morning and are able to have a happier, more active day.

Being proud of your achievements helps you to feel more confident.

How to increase exercise

Sixty minutes of exercise might sound like a long time, but if you spread it out over the whole day you will be surprised by how easy it can be. There are so many choices you can make.

Increasing exercise at home

Sometimes when we are at home, we are not very active. We may spend a lot of time watching TV, playing video games, or spending hours on the computer or on the phone – and of course there is always homework to be done! It's important to make time to play and be active.

Here are some great ideas to get active at home:

- Play a ball game.
- Go to the local tennis court.
- Go for a swim in the local pool.
- Go to a skate park.
- Take your dog for a walk.
- Go for a run.
- Try a new activity, such as a dance class.
- Ride your bike.
- Go for a walk.
- Go for a hike.
- Join a sporting club.
- Jump on a trampoline.
- Throw a frisbee.
- Complete jobs at home.

It is important to get outside each day and take part in a range of activities.

Increasing exercise at school

At school we get to join in physical education classes, which is a great opportunity to learn and improve skills and be active at school. We can also choose to be active at school during lunch break. There are lots of choices that will help us get our 60 minutes of exercise.

Try some of these activities:

- Play tag.
- Play a ball game with your friends.
- Have running races.
- Use a skipping rope.
- Ask a teacher to organise games at recess.
- Walk around the school with your friends, instead of sitting.
- Join a school sports team. (If your school doesn't have any, maybe you can start one!)
- Organise a 'Walk to School' day.

You probably have some other terrific ideas. Being active can be lots of fun, so go on – start enjoying yourself!

Don't forget about safety

Drink lots of water through the whole day, especially when you are active.

Be sun smart and wear a broad-brimmed hat, sunscreen, a shirt and sunglasses, and play in the shade. Wear the right protective gear, such as wearing a helmet when you ride your bike.

Drinking water is even more important when you're being active.

About medicines

Sometimes we get sick and a doctor will **prescribe** medicine. Medicine can be very helpful in getting us well again, but can be quite harmful if not used as directed.

When medicines can help us

When our body does not make enough of something that we need to stay healthy, we can use medicine to replace what is missing. This happens with type 1 diabetes, when the body does not make enough insulin.

Sometimes our body makes too much of something and that can make us sick. An example of this is Graves' disease, which is when the body makes too much thyroid hormone. Medicines can help stop this from happening.

Often when children get sick it is because of germs that get into the body. The body works hard to get rid of the germs, but this can make a person feel very unwell. Medicines can help the body get rid of the germs faster and build up the immune system.

Sometimes a person needs to take medicine for an illness that doesn't go away, such as asthma. Medicines can help control the illness and stop some of the worst symptoms from happening.

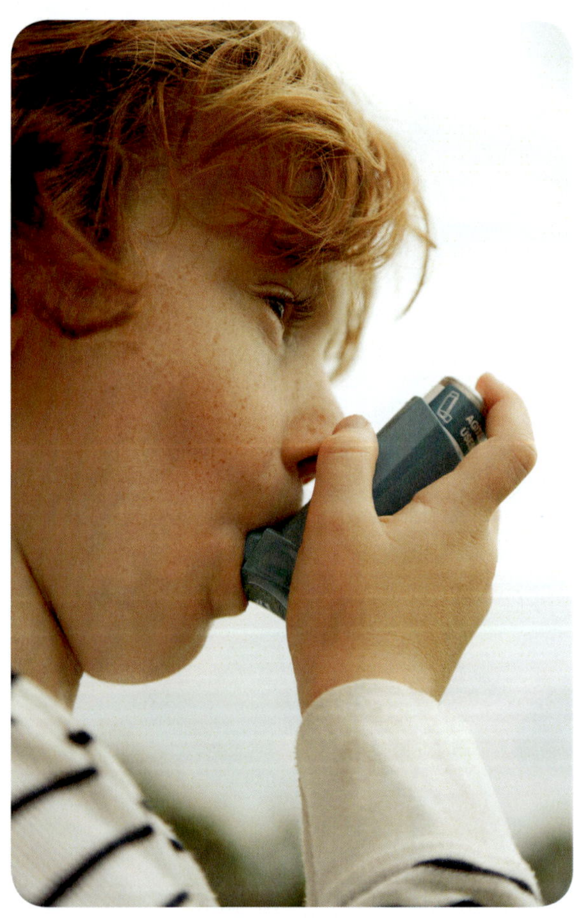

Managing asthma means taking control of your health and making sure that you are taking the correct medication in the right way.

Natural remedies

Sometimes medication is not required for small aches and pains. Headaches are a common symptom that people often take medicine for. Headaches can be caused by **dehydration**, skipping meals, being upset and crying, stress and worry, loud noises and stuffy rooms.

We can make choices to help **prevent** headaches:

- Drink plenty of water and have a healthy, balanced diet.
- Get plenty of fresh air.
- Be active every day.
- Get enough rest and sleep.

Did you know?

Australian Aboriginal people traditionally used plants and herbs to make medicines. To cure a headache, some groups used leaves from the Red Ash tree, crushing them in water. The liquid was then used to bathe the person.

If you need to take medication:

- make sure it is given by a trusted adult
- ask about the medication you are given
- check the dose you are given is correct
- make sure it has come from a package, not loose
- check the expiry date
- tell someone if the medication makes you feel odd or doesn't help you to feel better.

Make sure you always read the instructions and warnings on medicine containers.

When medicines can make us sick

Medicine can make people sick if the wrong medicine is taken, if they have a bad reaction to it or if too much is consumed. Sometimes people might offer you medicine that belongs to someone else because they think it will help you, but you should never take medicine that has been prescribed for someone else.

If you take the wrong medicine, or too much medicine, it can make you unwell or even lead to death. It is important to get help straight away. If a person becomes ill, call an ambulance (000).

If someone has taken the wrong medicine but feels fine, it is still important to get advice about what to do. You could call the Poisons Information Centre (131126). They are open all day and night.

There are helplines available if someone you know is ill, or has taken the wrong medicine.

Side-effects

All medicines can have side effects. It is important to make sure that the person who is giving you the medicine knows about the possible side effects, and what to do if you have a bad reaction.

Some side effects are minor, such as an upset stomach, and some can be more serious, requiring immediate medical attention. If a medicine makes you feel sick, tell an adult immediately, stop taking the medicine and, if there is no adult help, ring 000. You will be asked if you need police, the fire brigade or an ambulance. The relay officer will dial the correct service and stay on the line to talk to you.

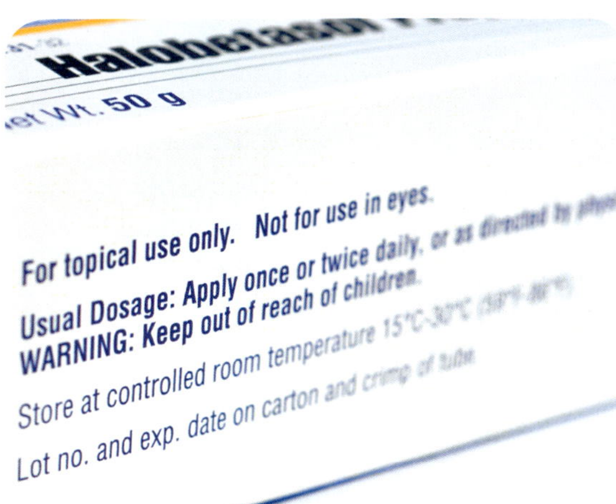

Always check the dosage listed on the medicine package before taking it.

Read all the information

It is important to read the information on medicine packages. It can give you very valuable information, including:

- what the active ingredient in the medicine is
- what the medicine is for
- how much medicine is in each pill or dose
- when you should *not* use the medicine at all
- when you should speak to your doctor before taking the medicine
- how much to use and how often to use it
- how it might make you feel
- when you should stop using the medicine
- things you shouldn't do while taking the medicine
- how to store the medicine.

Medicines should be stored in a safe place that cannot be reached by children, and kept in the bottle or box they came in *with the labels left on*. When a medicine is no longer needed, it can be taken to a **pharmacy** to be **disposed** of safely.

About tobacco

Tobacco is a plant and it is the main ingredient in cigarettes. Tobacco leaves are dried and broken into small pieces. Then a range of other products are added to the tobacco to make a cigarette. Cigarettes contain over 4000 chemicals – and many of them are poisonous. Many of these chemicals are released from the burning tobacco, while the rest come from the cigarette paper, **pesticides** on the tobacco and other chemicals that are added when a cigarette is made.

Tobacco plants

These chemicals are inhaled into the lungs. From there they go through the walls of the lungs into the bloodstream and are pumped all around the body. They can cause many diseases. Tar, nicotine and carbon monoxide are the cause of most smoking-related diseases.

Tar is a black, sticky substance that causes throat and lung cancer, as well as stains on the fingers, teeth and lungs. Tar has many poisonous chemicals.

Nicotine causes blood pressure to rise, and causes wrinkles. It is the main thing that makes people **addicted** to cigarettes.

Carbon monoxide is a poisonous gas that **reduces** the amount of oxygen in the blood, making the heart work harder to get oxygen to the body's organs.

Smoking a cigarette is like mixing up poisons from car exhaust fumes, pesticides, toilet cleaners, rat poison, lighter fluid, industrial solvents, insecticides, paint stripper, car batteries, rocket fuel and mothballs, and then inhaling them, all at the same time.

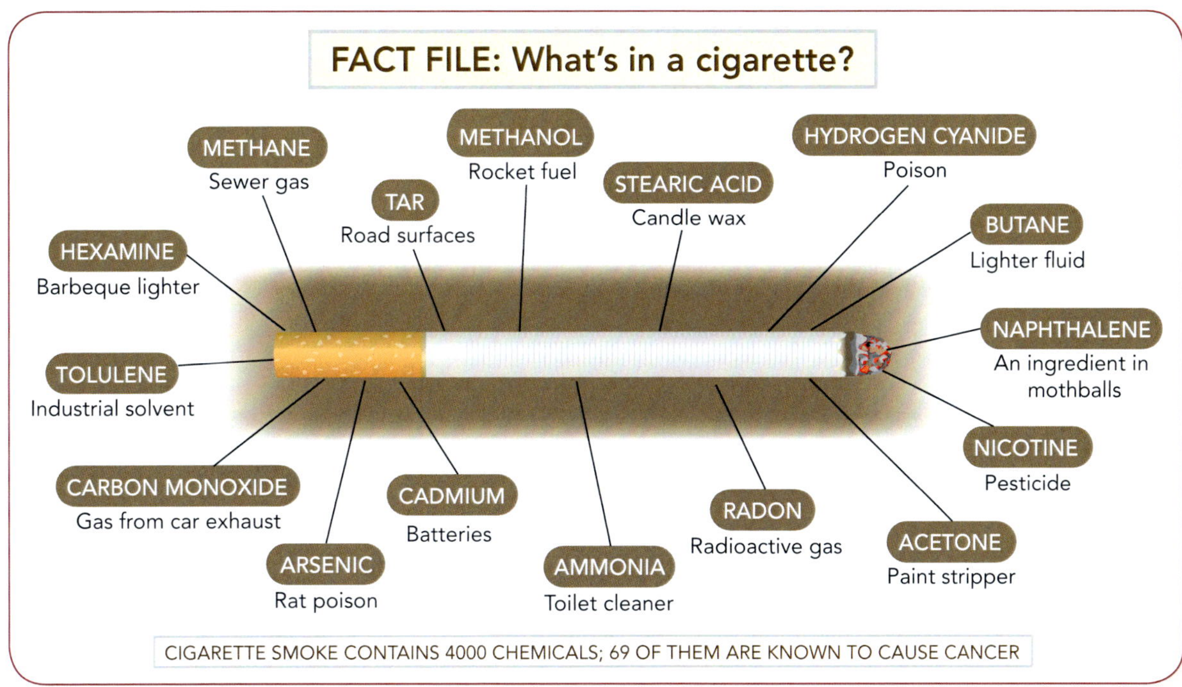

Short-term effects of smoking include:

- stained teeth and fingers
- smelly hair, breath and clothes
- more coughs and colds
- bad skin
- increased heart rate and blood pressure
- less oxygen to the lungs and brain
- difficulty in keeping fit
- shortage of money: cigarettes are very expensive!

Long-term effects of smoking include:

- cancer
- stroke
- blindness
- gum disease and loss of teeth
- heart disease
- heart attack
- emphysema
- stomach ulcers.

Smoking can cause so many diseases, but sometimes it is hard to think that far into the future. If you smoke when you are young, you are more likely to become a regular, heavy smoker. Most adult smokers wish they had never started and nearly all of them try to quit.

Second-hand smoke

If you are near someone who is smoking, there is a good chance you are breathing in the smoke from their cigarette. This is called second-hand or passive smoking, and it can make you unwell. You can even get diseases from second-hand smoke that cause death.

Second-hand smoking can cause you to have many of the problems that smokers have. Not only can the smell get in your hair and clothes, but it can make you cough and have breathing problems. You are more likely to have **respiratory** problems (such as pneumonia and bronchitis), ear infections, asthma, coughs and colds, and a higher chance of getting lung cancer and heart disease. The lungs of children who are exposed to second-hand smoke often develop slower. The risk of getting meningococcal disease is increased. Research has shown a link between second-hand smoking and childhood cancers.

Children are at risk of serious health effects from second-hand smoke. In most states in Australia, it is illegal to smoke in cars carrying children.

Here are some choices you can make to keep yourself safe from second-hand smoke:

- Ask people not to smoke when they are near you, especially indoors or in a car (remember to do this politely).
- Move away from someone who is smoking.
- Remind people who smoke that when they smoke, they cause harm to other people as well as to themselves.
- If people in your family smoke, ask if your home can be a smoke-free zone.

Clean Air Zone

For the health and safety of our community, there is no smoking in our buildings, at our entrances or on our grounds.

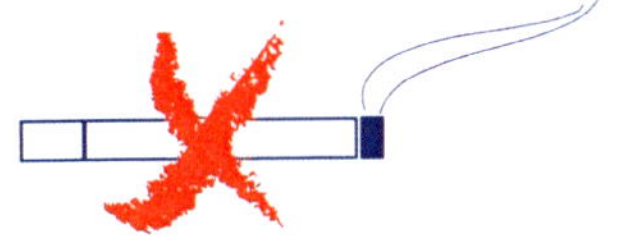

Put up a sign to establish your own Clean Air Zone.

Each Australian state and territory has laws about where people can and cannot smoke. Most states and territories have laws banning smoking in cars when there are children present.

Did you know?

Approximately 290 people die from smoking every week. Smoking is the cause of most drug-related deaths. When people stop smoking, their bodies begin to repair themselves; within a day nicotine is out of their bloodstream; in a week, lungs start to recover; and in a year, people are less stressed and can breathe more easily.

Many workplaces and venues across Australia have banned smoking.

About alcohol

Alcohol is a drug. When someone swallows alcohol, it goes from the mouth to the stomach and small intestine. Then it passes through the walls of the stomach and small intestine and enters the bloodstream very quickly. It travels in the blood to the brain and it slows down and changes the way messages are sent to and from the brain.

Like many drugs, alcohol can make it hard for someone to think, speak and see things the way they really are.

Alcohol has different effects on different people, depending on the amount that is consumed. It can make them do things they wouldn't usually do. Normal judgement is changed, and people can make unsafe choices when they are affected by alcohol.

Alcohol slows down reflexes and makes people less coordinated. Sometimes people feel dizzy and fall down. Sometimes they have much more serious accidents and can injure themselves.

Excessive consumption of alcohol can cause blurred vision, slurred speech and slower reflexes.

After drinking too much alcohol, a person's speech can become slurred and their vision become blurry. They can feel very tired. Often people get a headache and feel sick, or even vomit. Some people may even blackout. In more serious cases, people can go into a coma and even die.

People who are under the **influence** of alcohol can become very **aggressive** and fight with other people. They may fight with their family, their friends or the police. Sometimes they lose their friends because their friends don't like the way they are behaving.

It is common for people to feel very embarrassed and ashamed of the things they did while they were under the influence of alcohol.

People who drink a lot of alcohol can become addicted to alcohol. It can also lead to liver damage and brain damage. People who drink too much alcohol are at higher risk of having a stroke. It can also lead to depression, problems with school and work, and family and friendship problems.

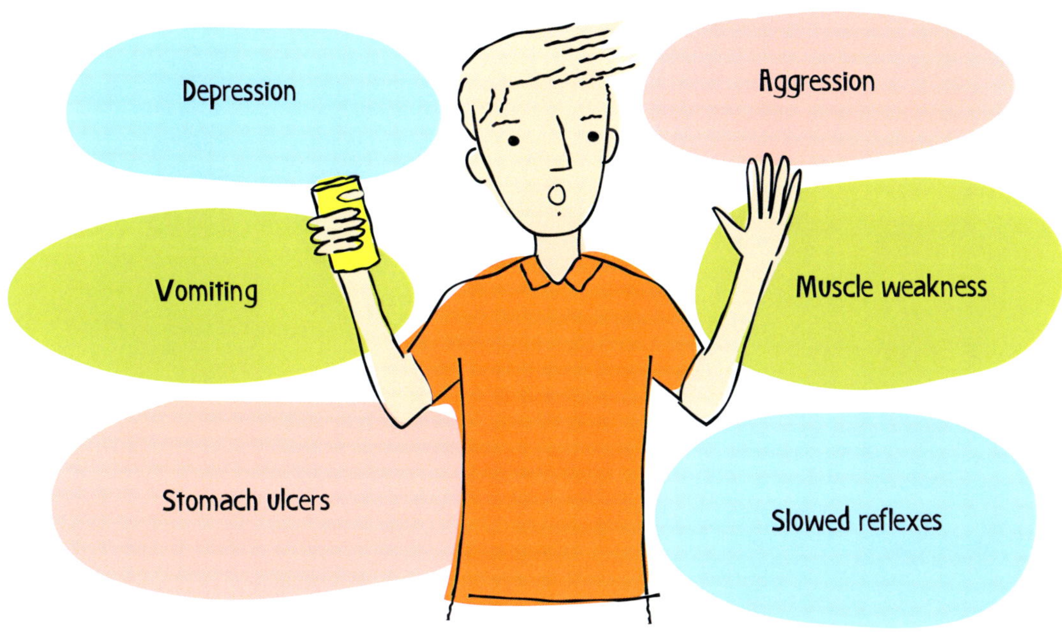

If alcohol is consumed in excess, it is likely to cause a range of health problems.

Is there a 'safe' amount of alcohol?

The way alcohol affects people depends on many things, including whether they are male or female, their age, their weight, how much they have had to eat, how they are feeling and any other medicines they may have taken.

There are Australian Government guidelines for healthy adults, to reduce the risk of alcohol-related harm. These guidelines have been developed by the National Health and Medical Research Council.

The guidelines are as follows:

- To reduce the risk of alcohol-related harm over a lifetime, drink no more than two standard drinks on any day.
- To reduce the risk of injury from a single occasion of drinking, drink no more than four standard drinks.
- There is no safe amount of alcohol for children. The only safe amount is none.

Did you know?

In Australia, a standard drink is a drink that contains 10 grams of alcohol.

The amount of alcohol in drinks and bottles varies.

1.4
375 ml
Full strength
4.8% Alc. Vol

1
375 ml
Mid strength
3.5% Alc. Vol

0.8
375 ml
Low strength
2.7% Alc. Vol

What happens when children and teenagers drink alcohol?

When children or teenagers drink alcohol, it can affect the way their brain grows and develops. It especially affects memory, motor skills (ability to move) and coordination.

Children or teenagers who drink alcohol can get alcohol poisoning more easily than an adult. This is very serious and can lead to serious health conditions and – in the worse case – even death.

Like adults, children or teenagers who drink alcohol are more likely to take risks or behave badly. This can lead to accidents and fights. Because alcohol alters body perception and coordination, it can cause serious injuries, and inappropriate responses.

Did you know?

Alcohol is the drug that causes the most drug-related deaths in teenagers. On average, four Australians under the age of 25 die each week from alcohol-related injuries

Keep yourself safe

If someone is drinking alcohol, you can make some choices to keep yourself safe:

- Stay away from someone who has drunk too much alcohol.
- Stay close to an adult you trust if people around you are drinking alcohol.
- Get help from an adult if you feel that you are in danger from someone who has drunk too much alcohol.
- Never get in a car if the driver has been drinking alcohol.

How to say 'no'

As you get older, you are more likely to have to make choices about alcohol, cigarettes, medicines and other drugs. Sometimes you may be offered something that is not meant for you or is not good for you. It is important to know your rights and remember that you have choices and you can say 'no'.

Friends might try to force you to do something you don't want to do. This is called peer pressure and it is not OK. They might say things like "Come on, everyone else does it," or "You are so uncool!" Or they might just laugh at you.

It is not true that everyone makes bad or unsafe choices. In fact, most people usually make good choices.

Saying 'no' to something doesn't mean you are scared. It means you have **respect** for your body and care about your health. Smoking, drinking alcohol or taking things that are not meant for you are considered 'risk-taking behaviours' and they not only affect your health, they could affect your future dreams, too.

Saying 'no' can be hard, especially if someone is pressuring you to do something.

There are different ways you can say 'no'. Here are some you could try:

- Just say 'no, thanks'. Sometimes this isn't as hard as we think it is going to be, and if the person is a friend, they will respect your decision.
- If 'no' doesn't work the first time, you could try saying it over and over again. This way, the person will eventually get the idea and give up asking you.
- Sometimes it is best to move away from the person. Say 'no' and walk away. This can be one of the best ways to **refuse** something.
- Try changing the subject. Maybe you could suggest another activity. For example, "No, thanks. Let's go and shoot some hoops," or "Let's go to my place," or "I really want to try out my new game".

- Be honest. "No, thanks. I don't like what it does to people and I don't want it."
- You could try being funny. "No thanks. It kills your brain cells and I need all I can get!" "I don't want to have bad breath and stink."
- Use an excuse that will get you away from the situation. For example, "Mum just rang and I have to go home," or "I've got basketball training this afternoon," or "I've got to go, I'm meeting up with some friends".

It's a great idea to choose a few of these options that you think will work for you. Some options will work better for some people than others. Once you have decided what is best for you, talk about it and practise it with your family. That way you can gain some confidence in your decision-making.

Did you know?
Young people who have hobbies, exercise, play sport or study hard are less likely to abuse alcohol or other drugs.

Practise different scenarios with your family, so that you get some confidence in your own decision-making.

Tips for when you say 'no'

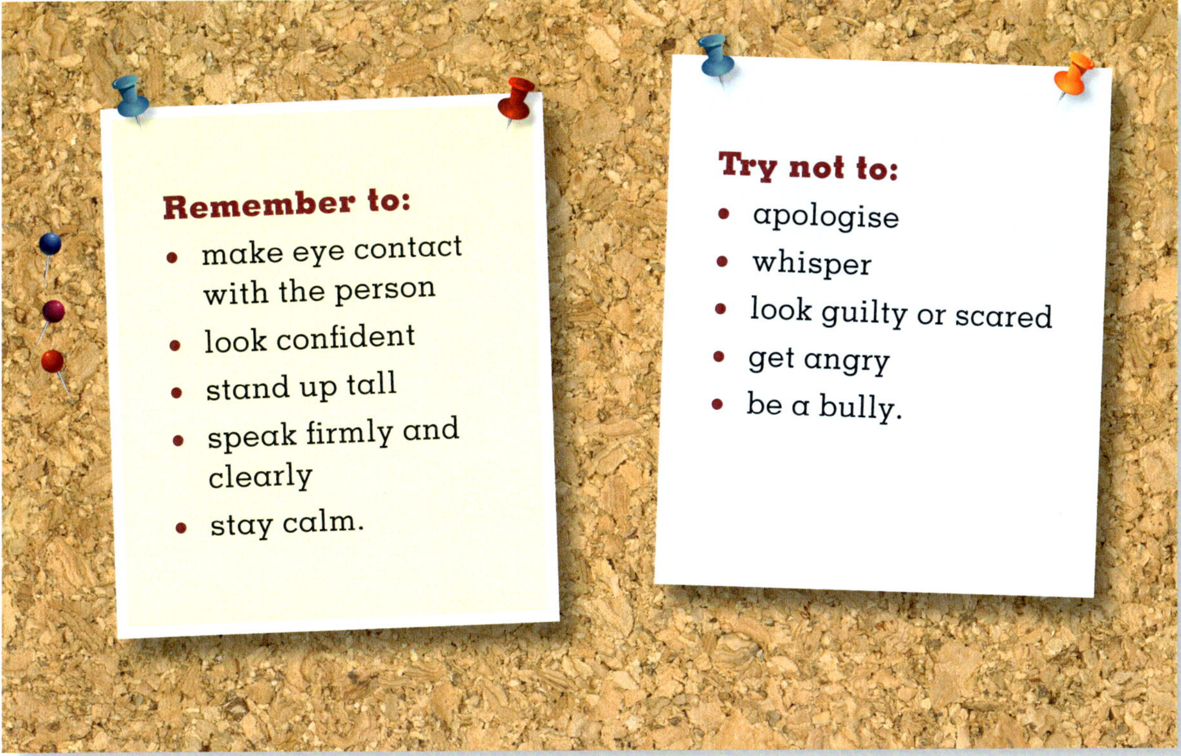

There are times and places where you are more likely to be pressured to do things you don't want to do. During those times, it's important to think about your health and safety. Be confident and avoid harmful risk-taking. Try to surround yourself with other people who make good choices. If all your friends make bad choices, it is harder to keep making good choices.

If you have any questions, remember that you can ask a parent or other adults. Often, adults will have experienced similar situations and can give you some insight.

By saying 'no' to unsafe choices, you are also saying 'yes' to more healthy choices. You are setting a great example for your friends, and your family will be proud of you for making good decisions. Sometimes it can be difficult watching friends make poor choices. You can give advice, but individuals ultimately make their own decisions.

Connections

Choices we make can affect our lives in many different ways. As we get older, the types of decisions we are faced with change. We become responsible for more and more of our choices.

We have looked at many of the things that might affect our health and safety, but there are many others, such as cyber safety, being safe around traffic and staying safe in the water. Be aware of the risks around you and things you can do to reduce your chance of being hurt or becoming sick.

Choices that keep us healthy and safe when we are young will improve our chances of becoming a healthy and strong adult. Poor choices can affect our dreams and goals, our families and our friends.

Find out all your options and the possible consequences of your choices, and think carefully about the decisions you make. Be confident when you make choices and don't let other people encourage you to make poor choices.

Remember, you do have choices and it's up to you to make the best choices for you.

Make friends with other people who make good choices.

Glossary

achievements done through effort

addicted unable to stop

aggressive being forceful or showing readiness to attack

allergies abnormal reactions to things that are not harmful to most people

comparing looking carefully at two (or more) things to find similarities and differences

concentrate to give your attention to something

consequences things that happen as a result of an action

dehydration losing too much water from your body

dietary the kinds and amounts of food eaten

disposed to get rid of

function perform, work

improves becomes better

influence something that affects someone or something without any direct force

lean little or no fat

nutrients parts of food that help you live and be healthy

nutrition the act or process of getting things that help you live and be healthy

pesticides chemicals used to kill animals or insects that damage plants or crops

pharmacy a shop where medicines are prepared and sold

prescribe given as a remedy by a doctor

prevent stop

recommendation a suggestion about what should be done

reduces makes smaller

refuse to say or show that you don't want to do or accept something

respect to admire someone or something

respiratory related to breathing

stressed very worried or anxious

Index